Wildlife through the Branches

Coloring Book

Copyright © 2012

Deborah S. Huffman

All rights reserved.

ISBN: 1977571328
ISBN-13: 9781977571328

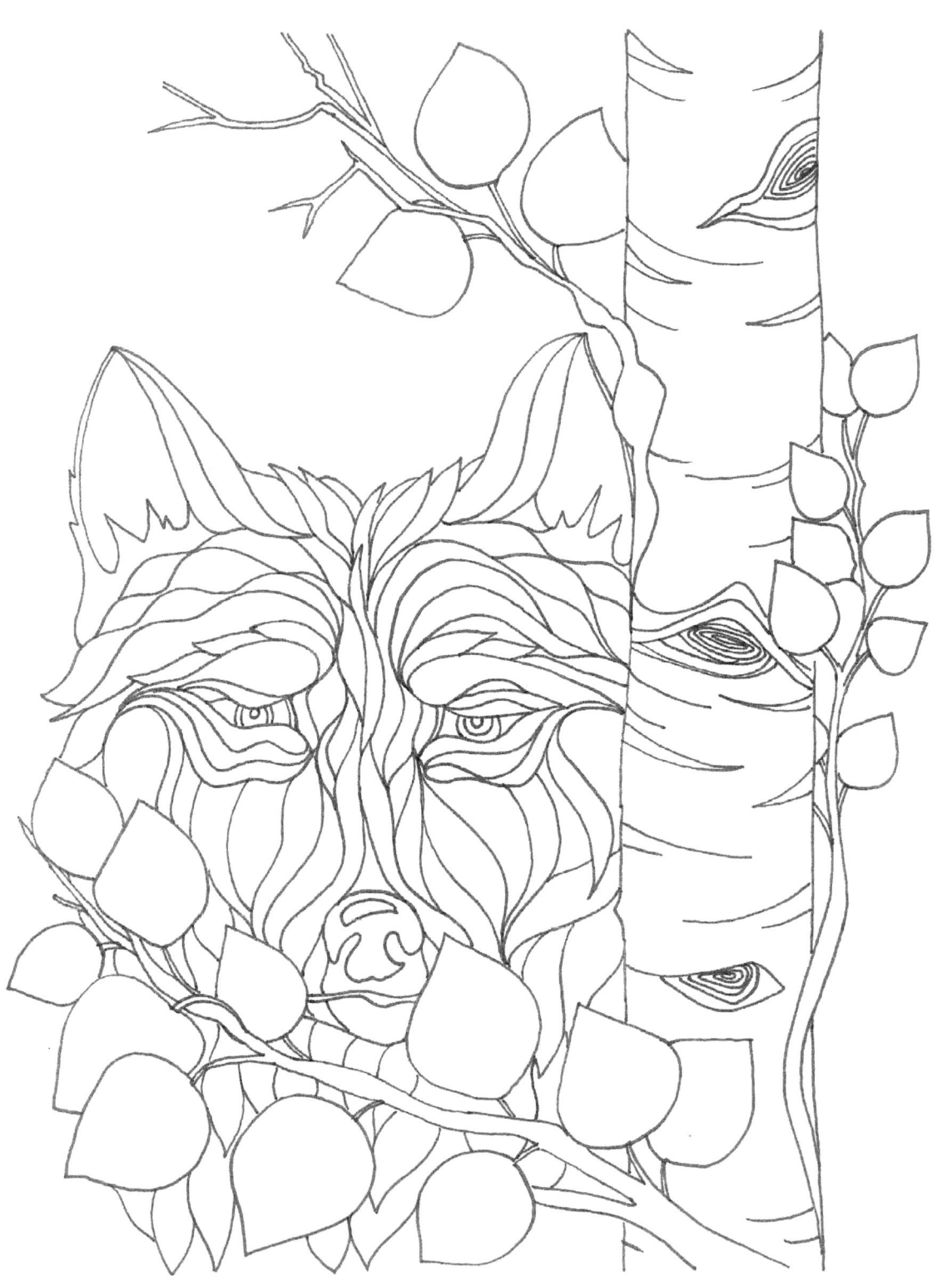

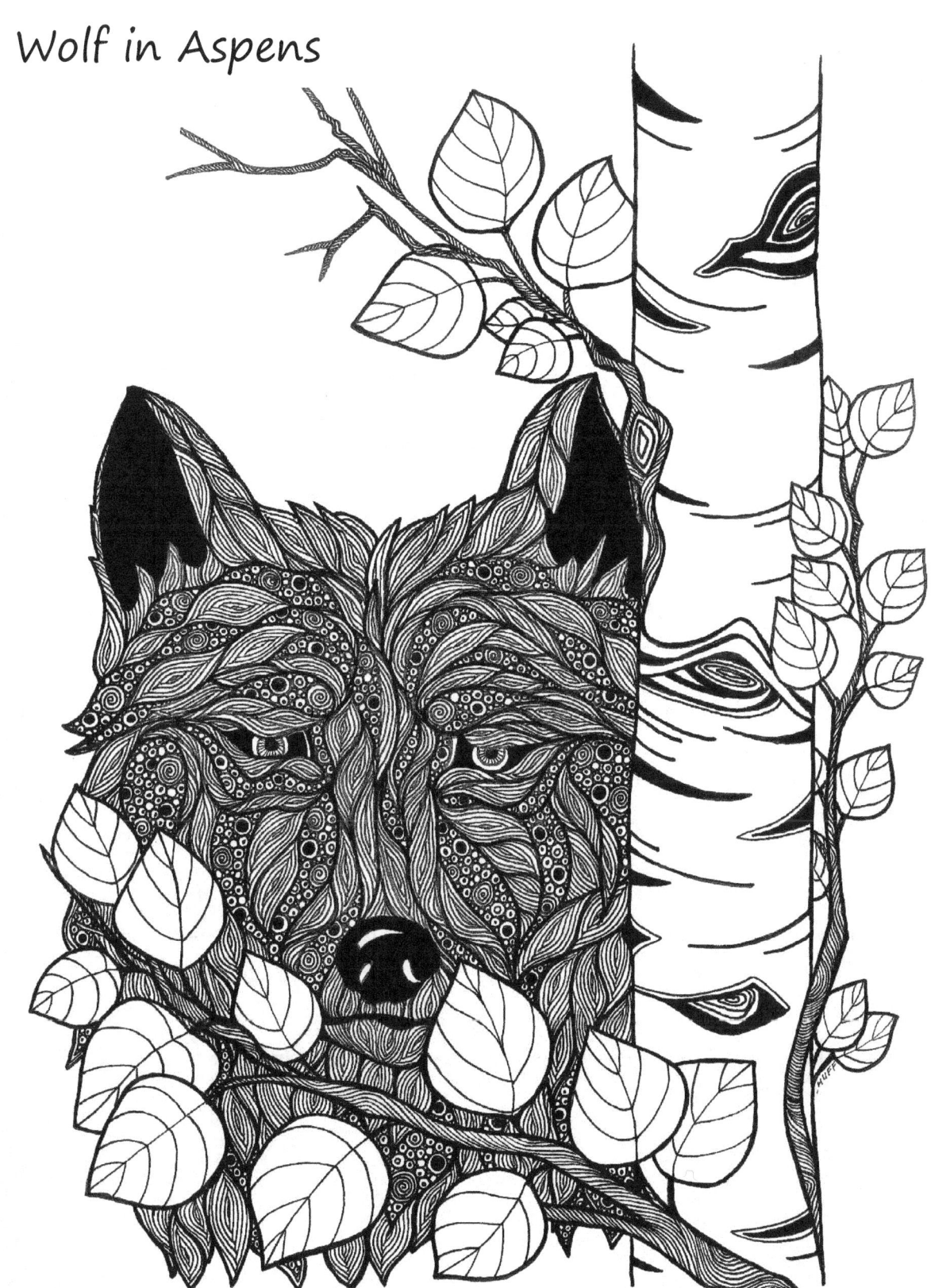

Wolf in Aspens

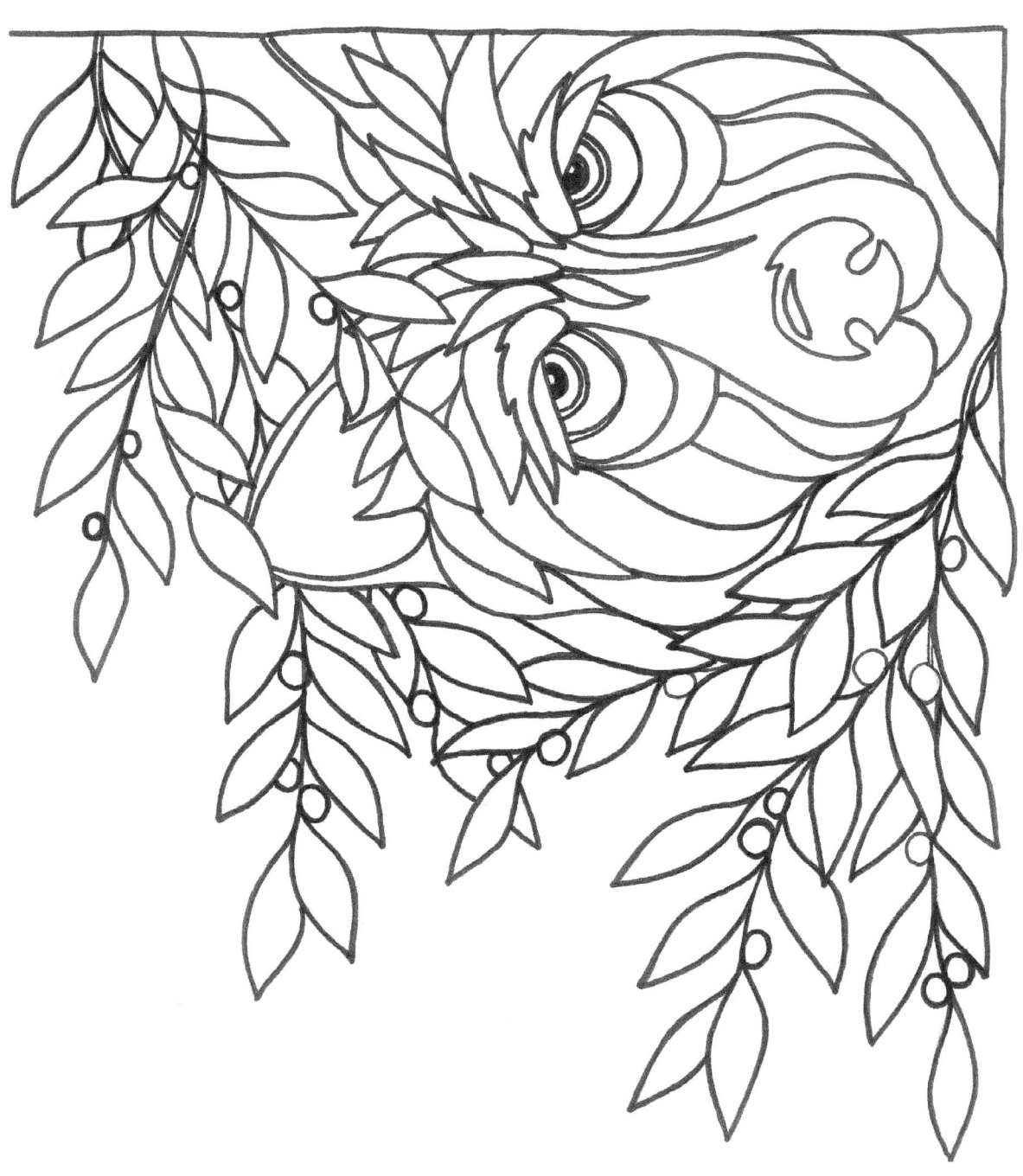

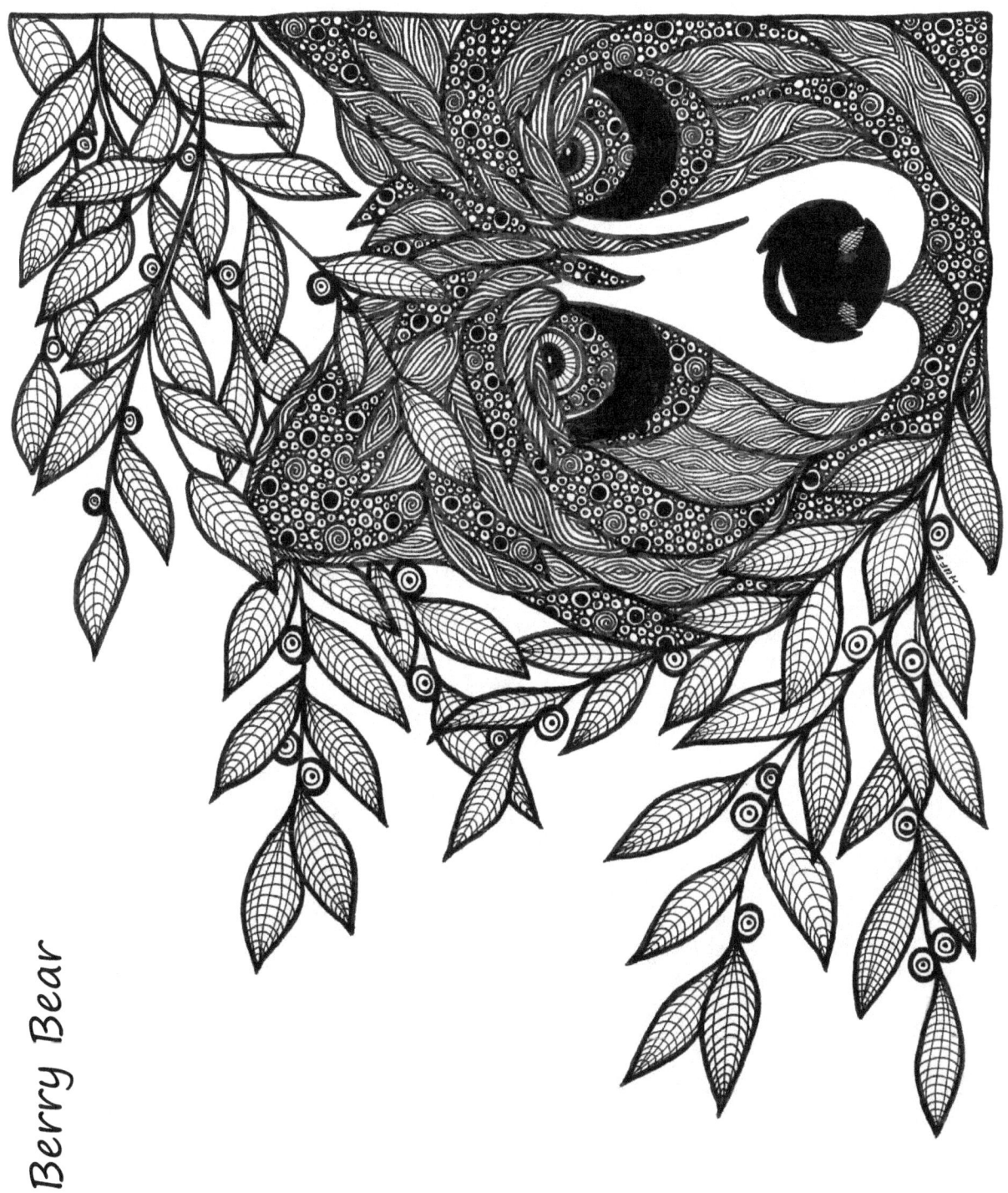

Berry Bear

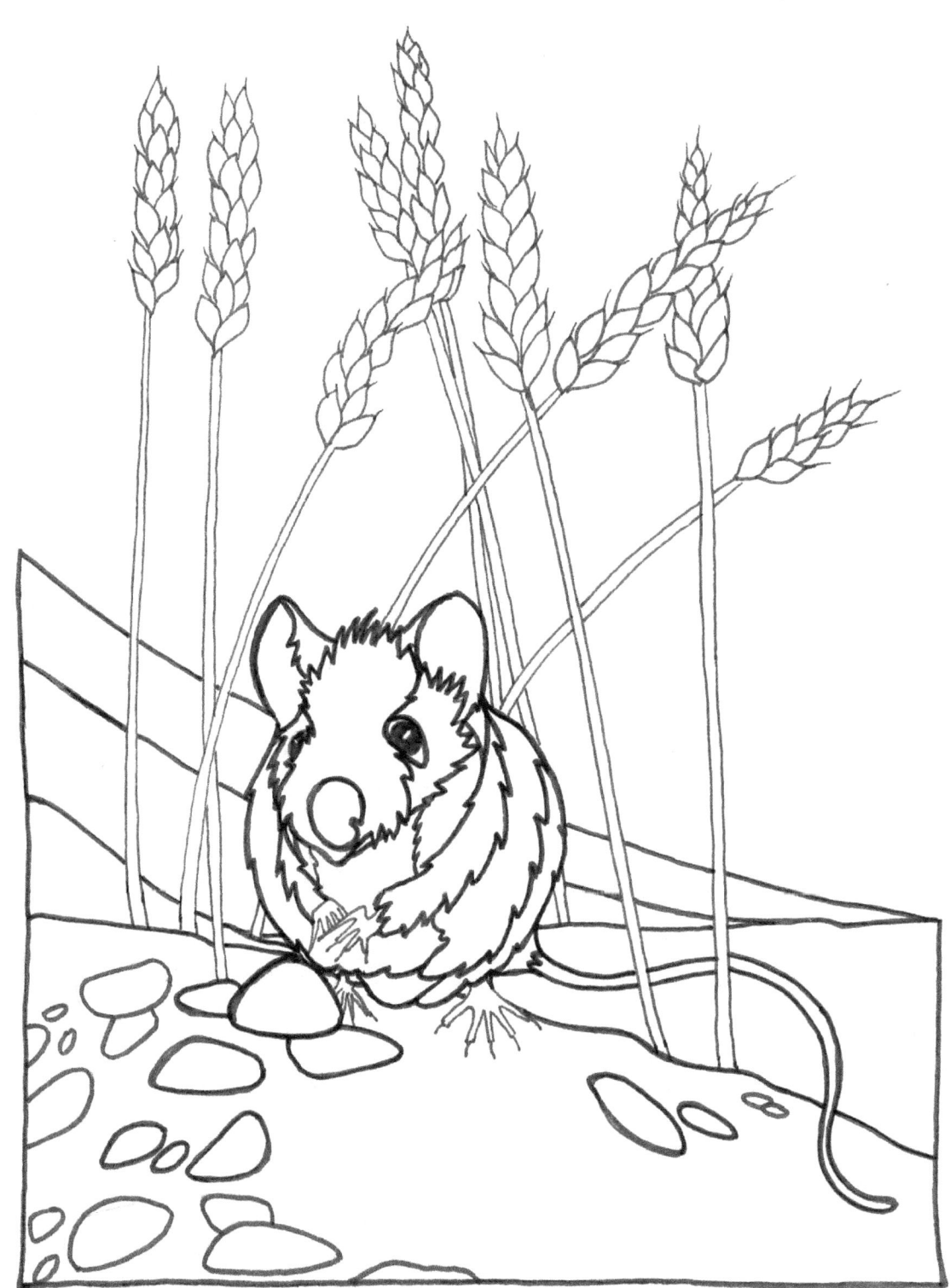

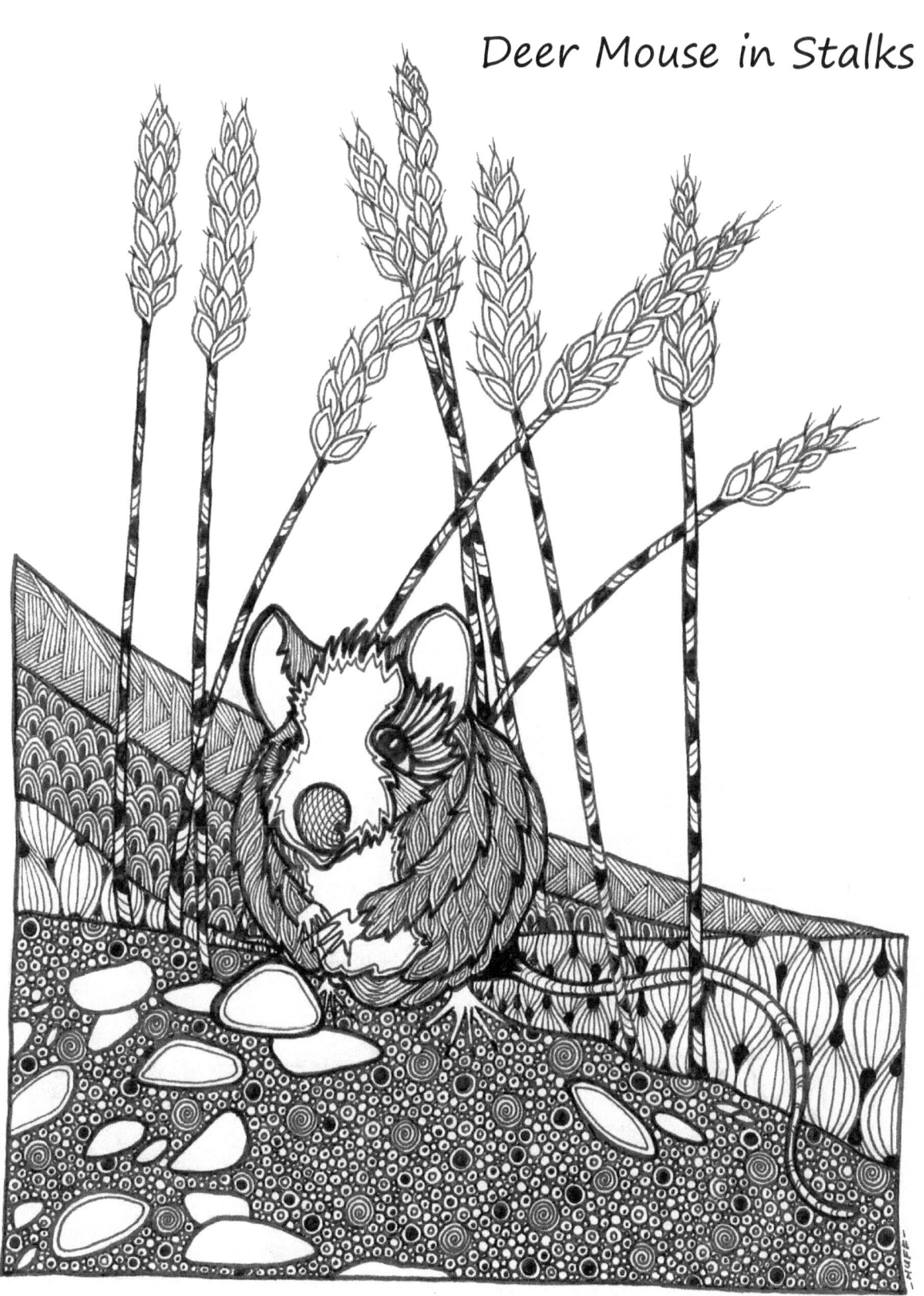

Deer Mouse in Stalks

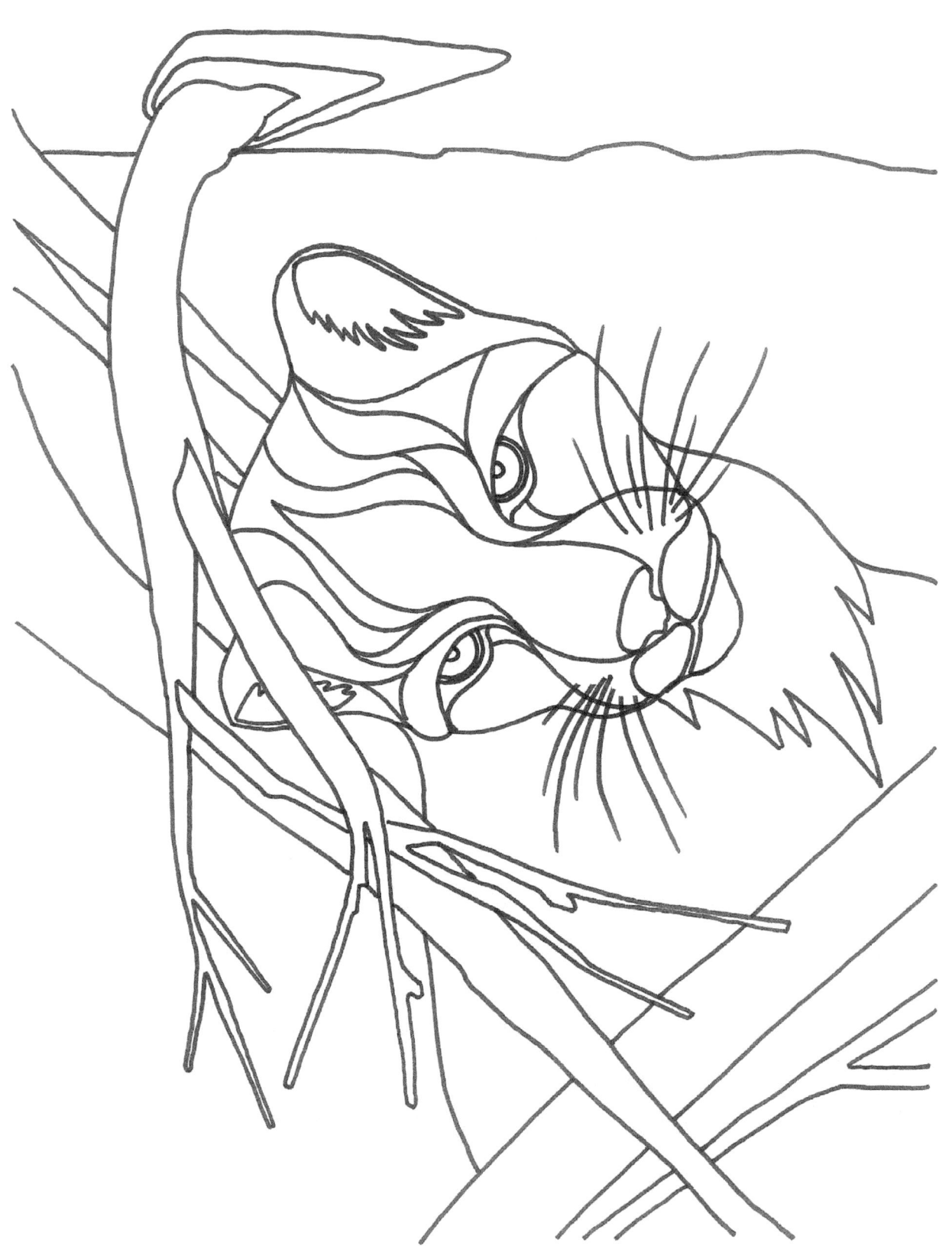

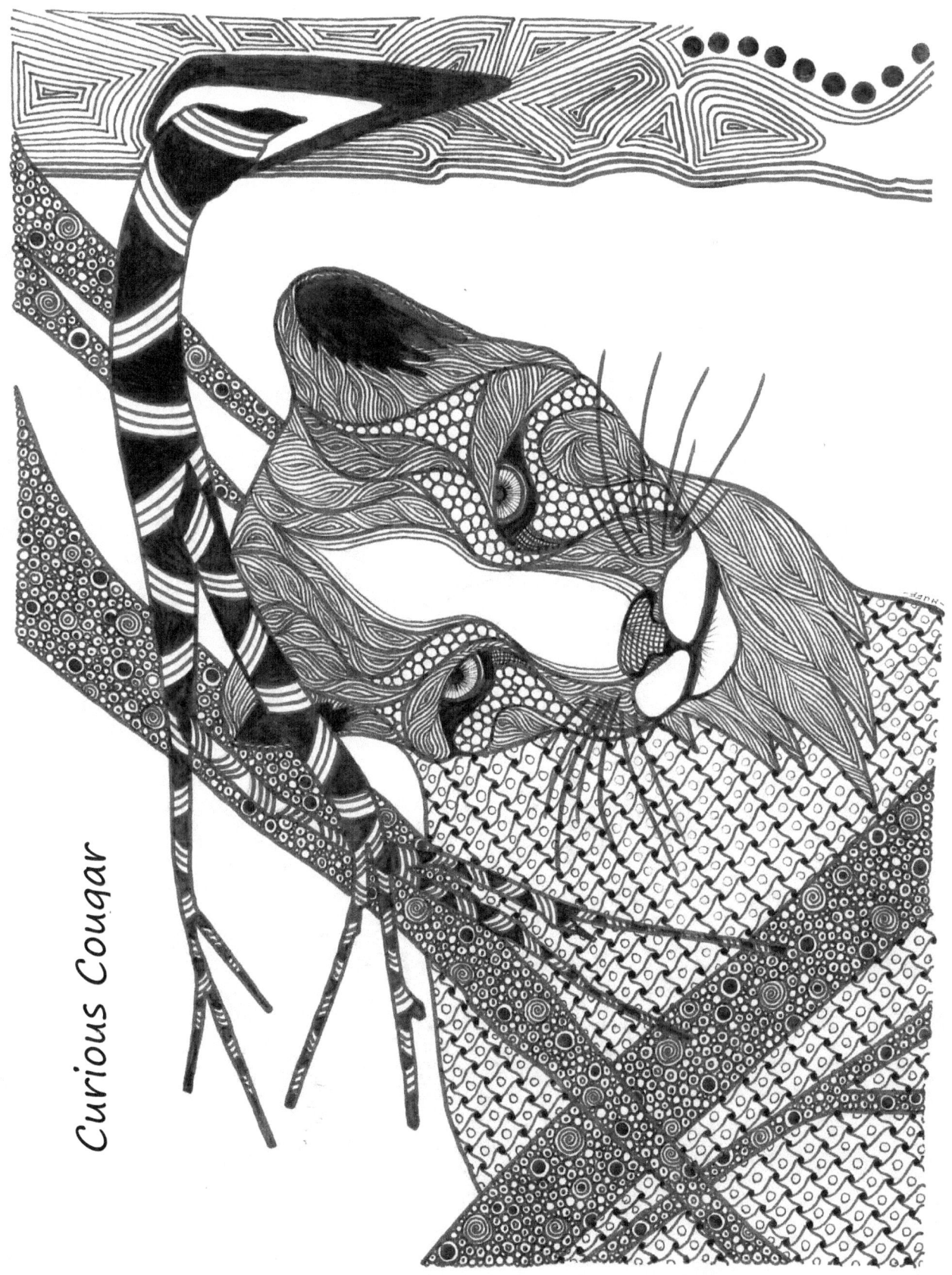

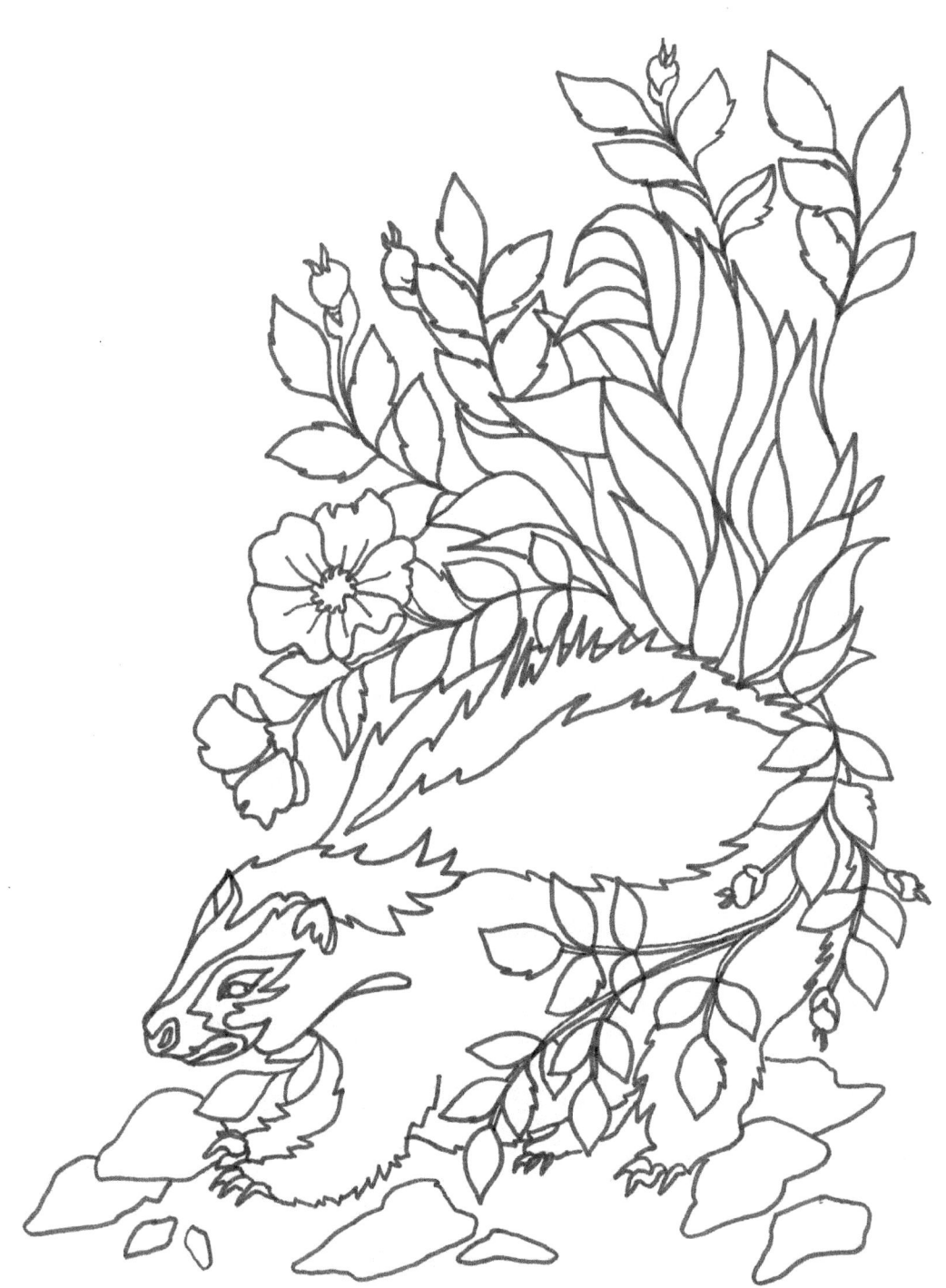

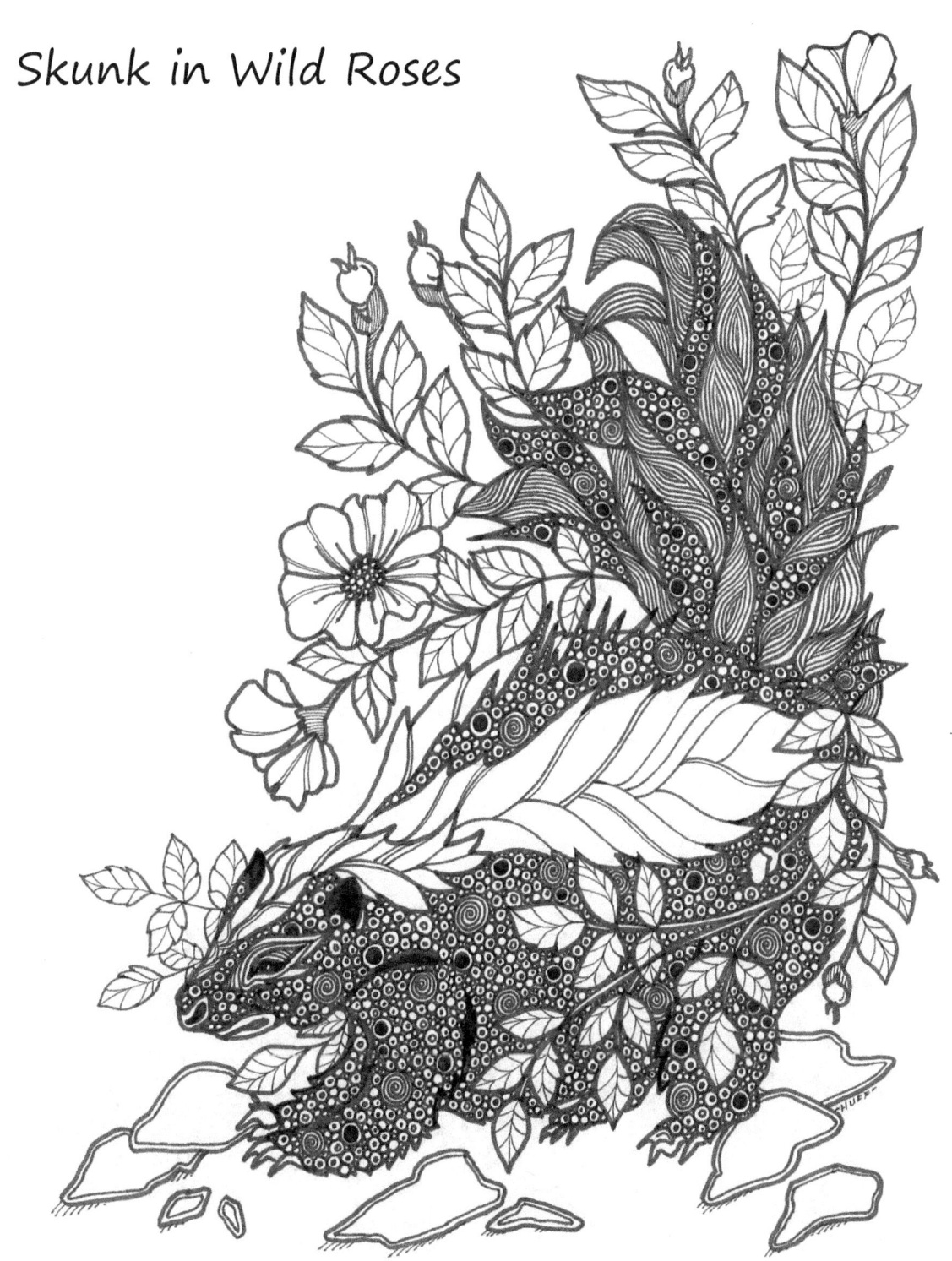

Skunk in Wild Roses

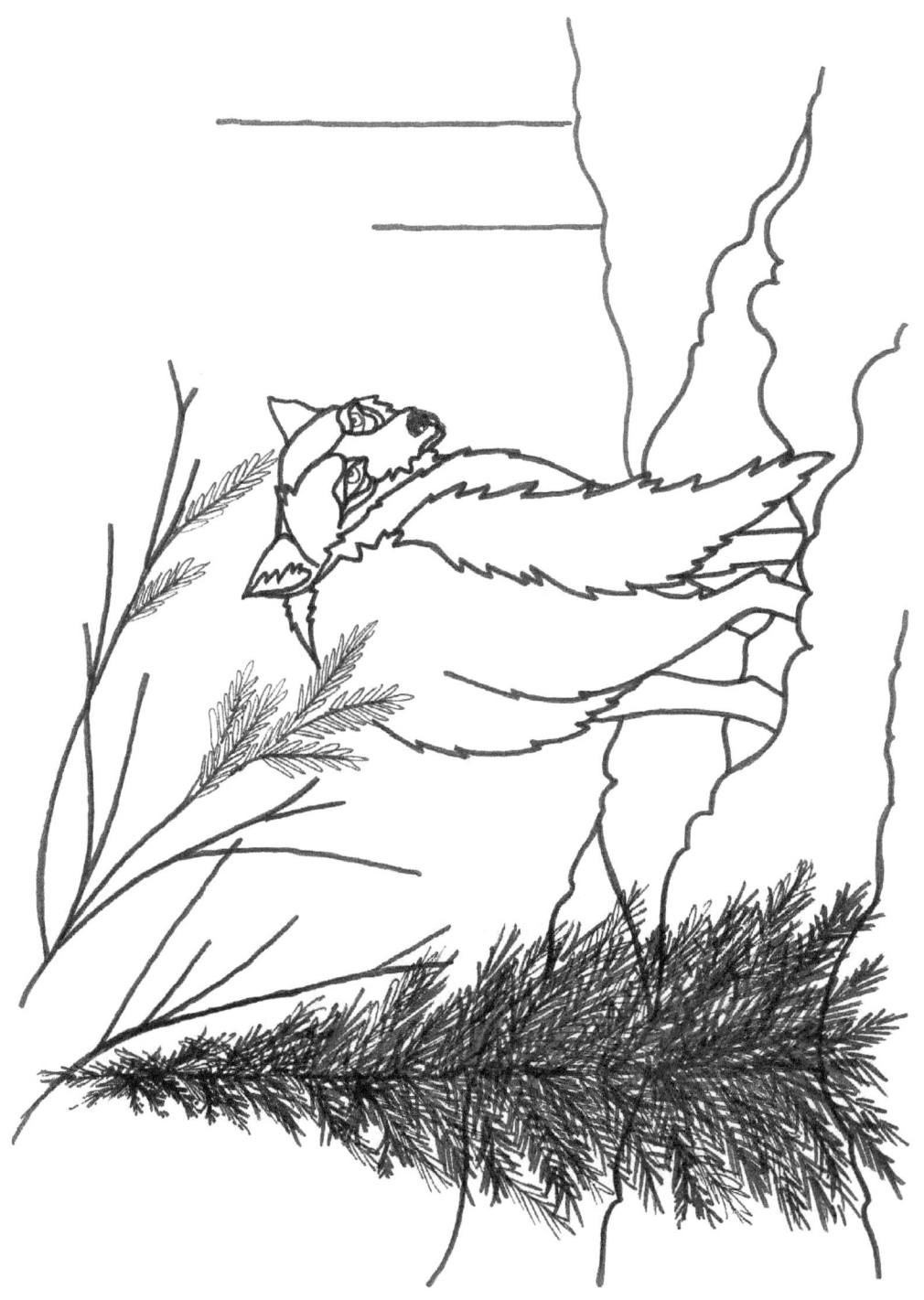

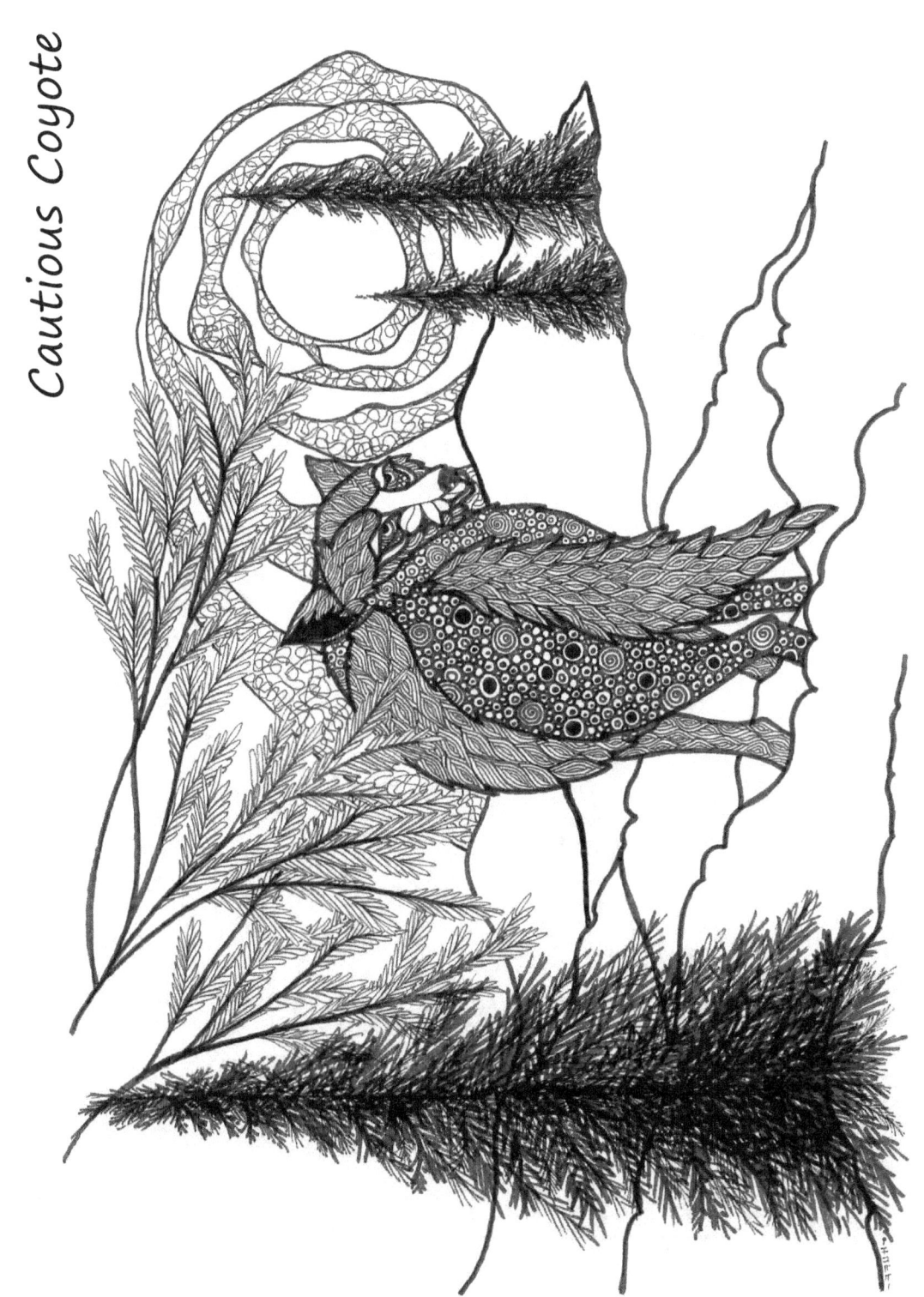

Cautious Coyote

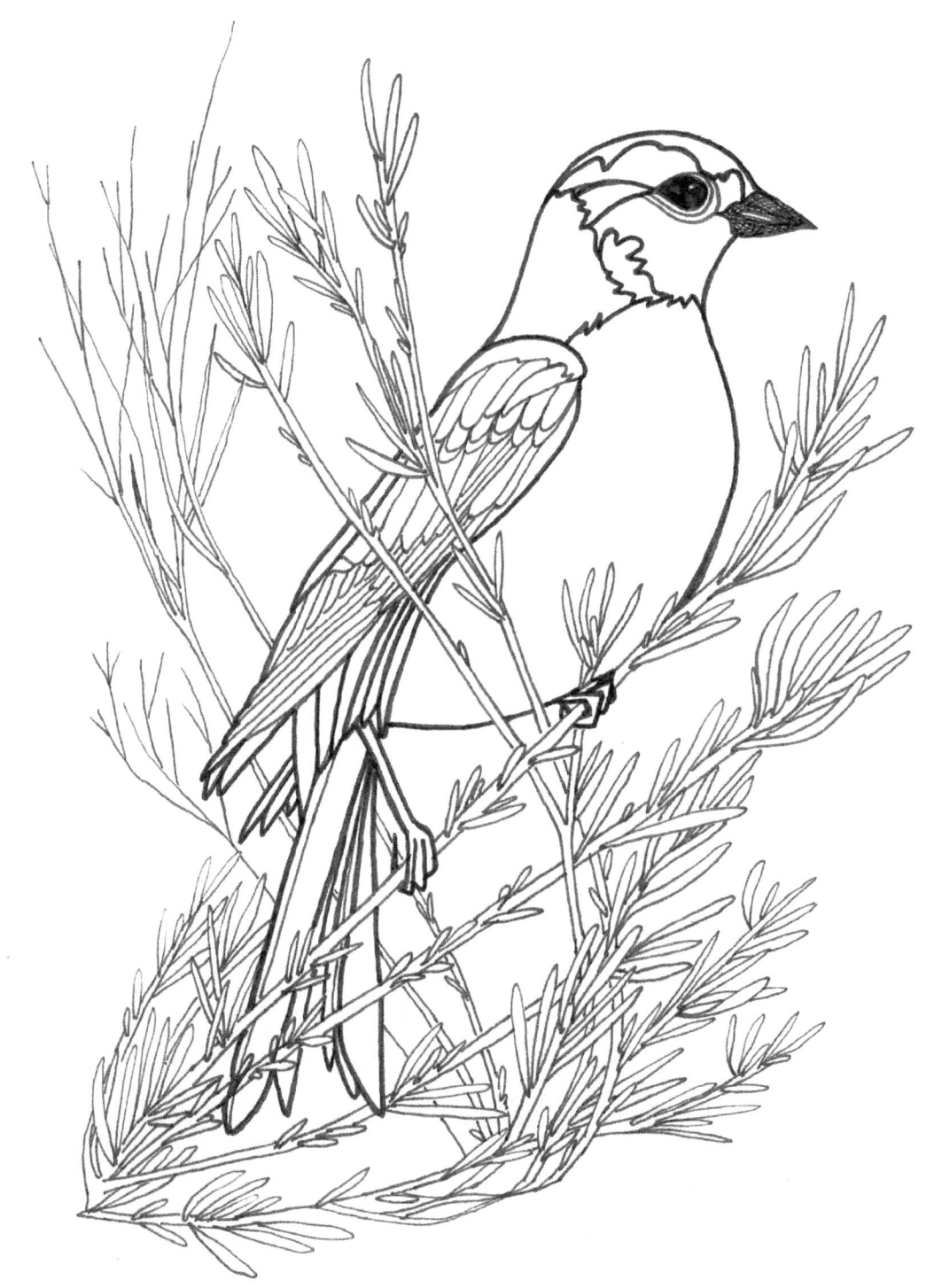

Chestnut Collared Longspur

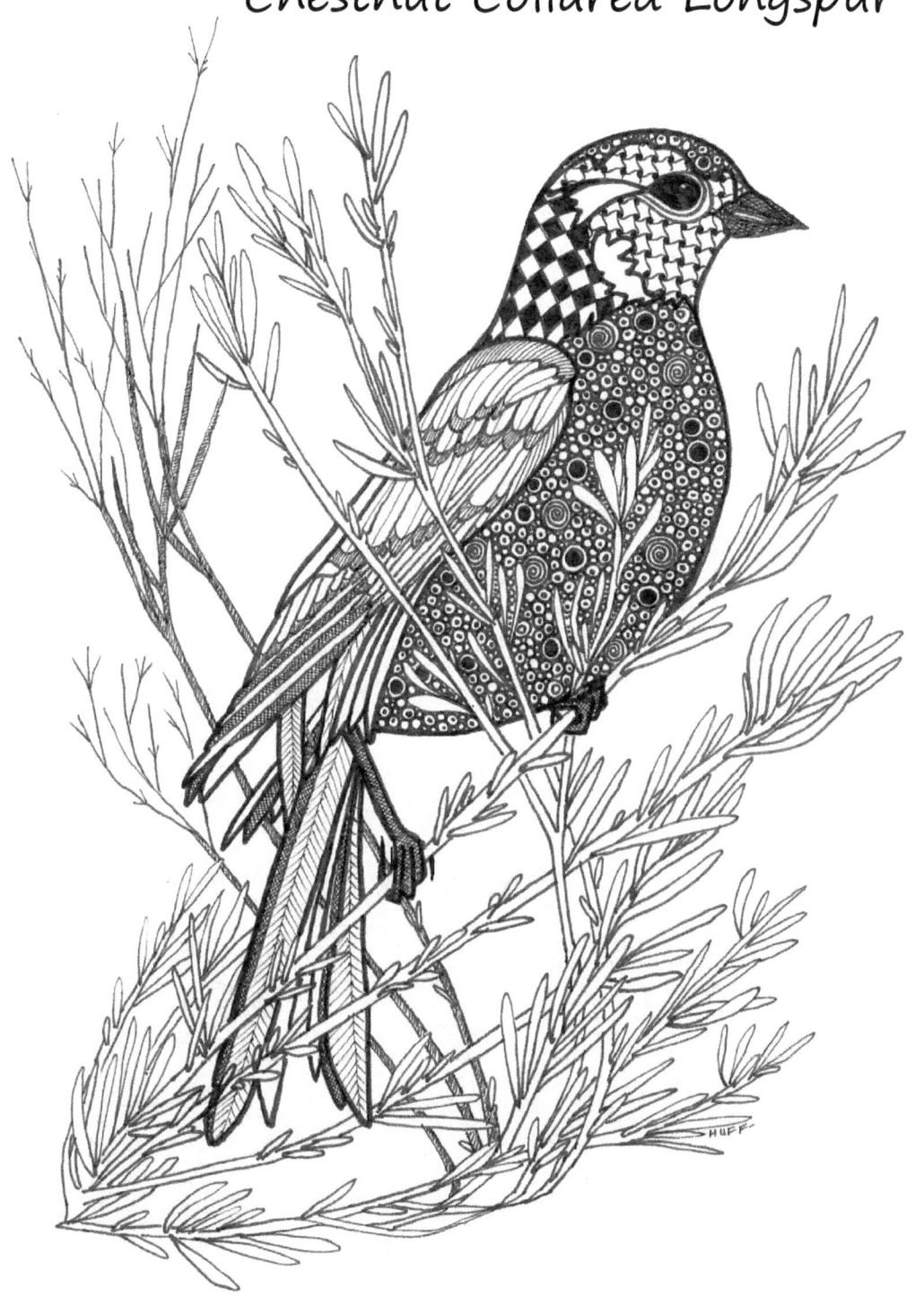

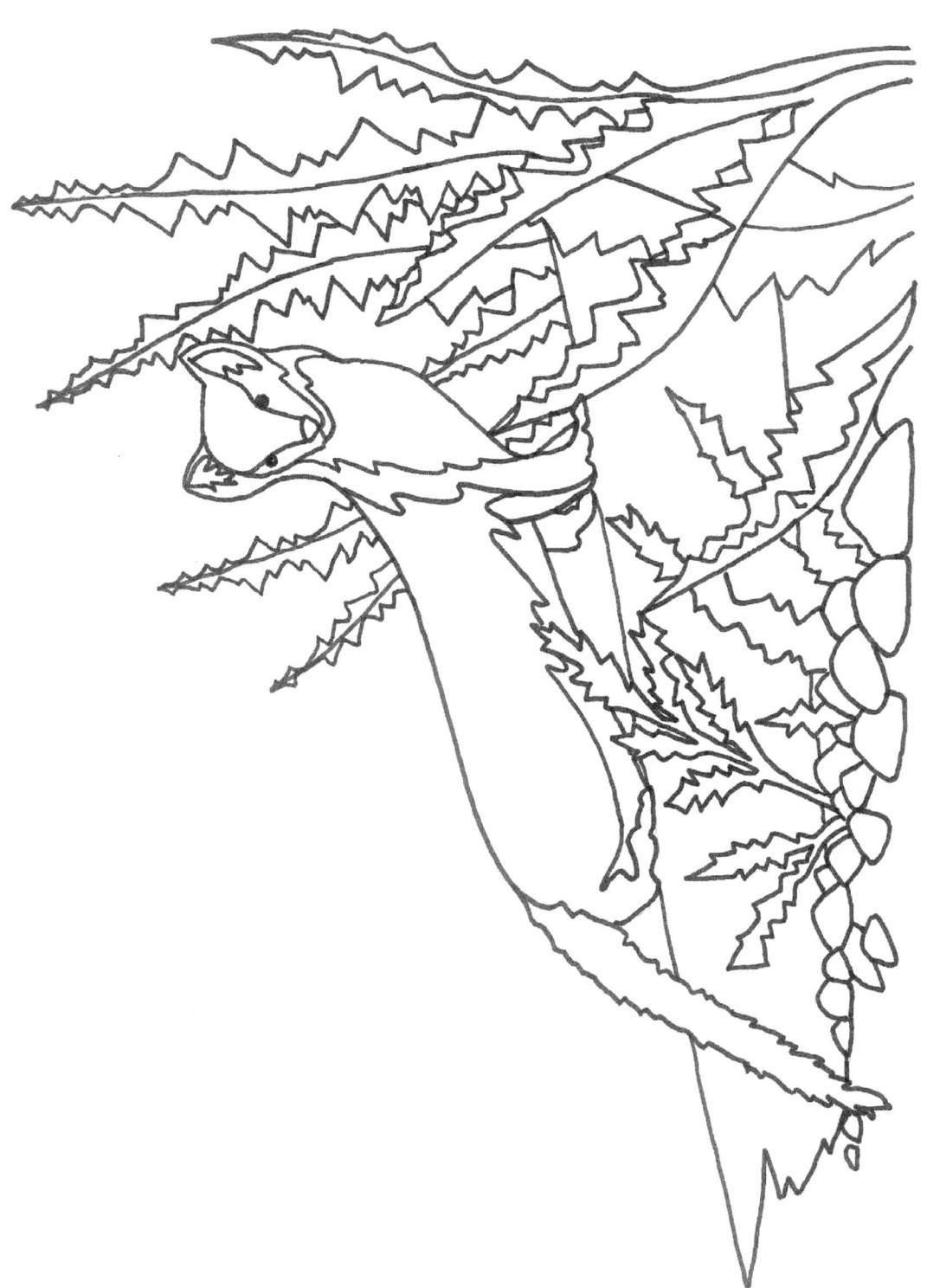

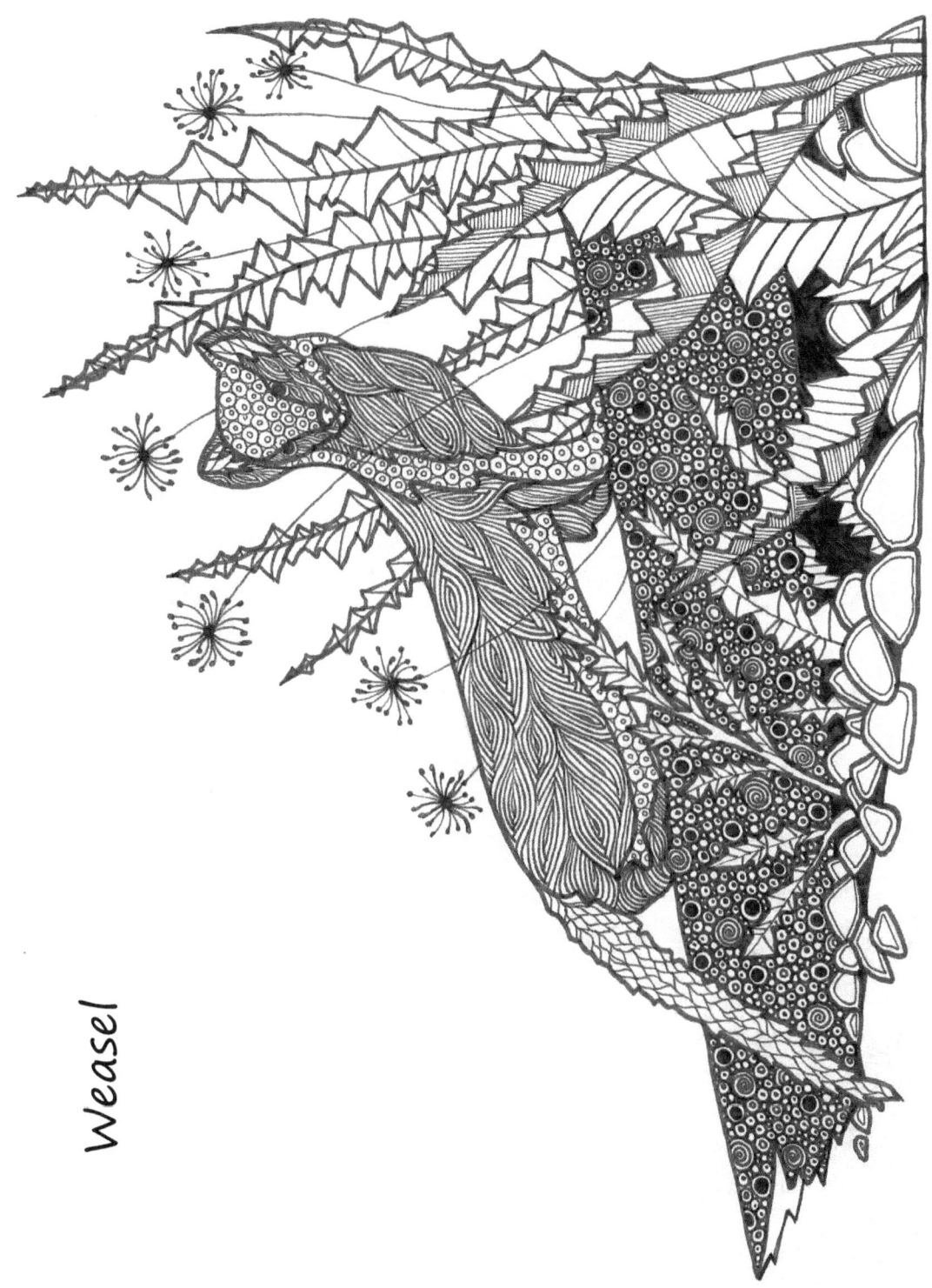

Weasel

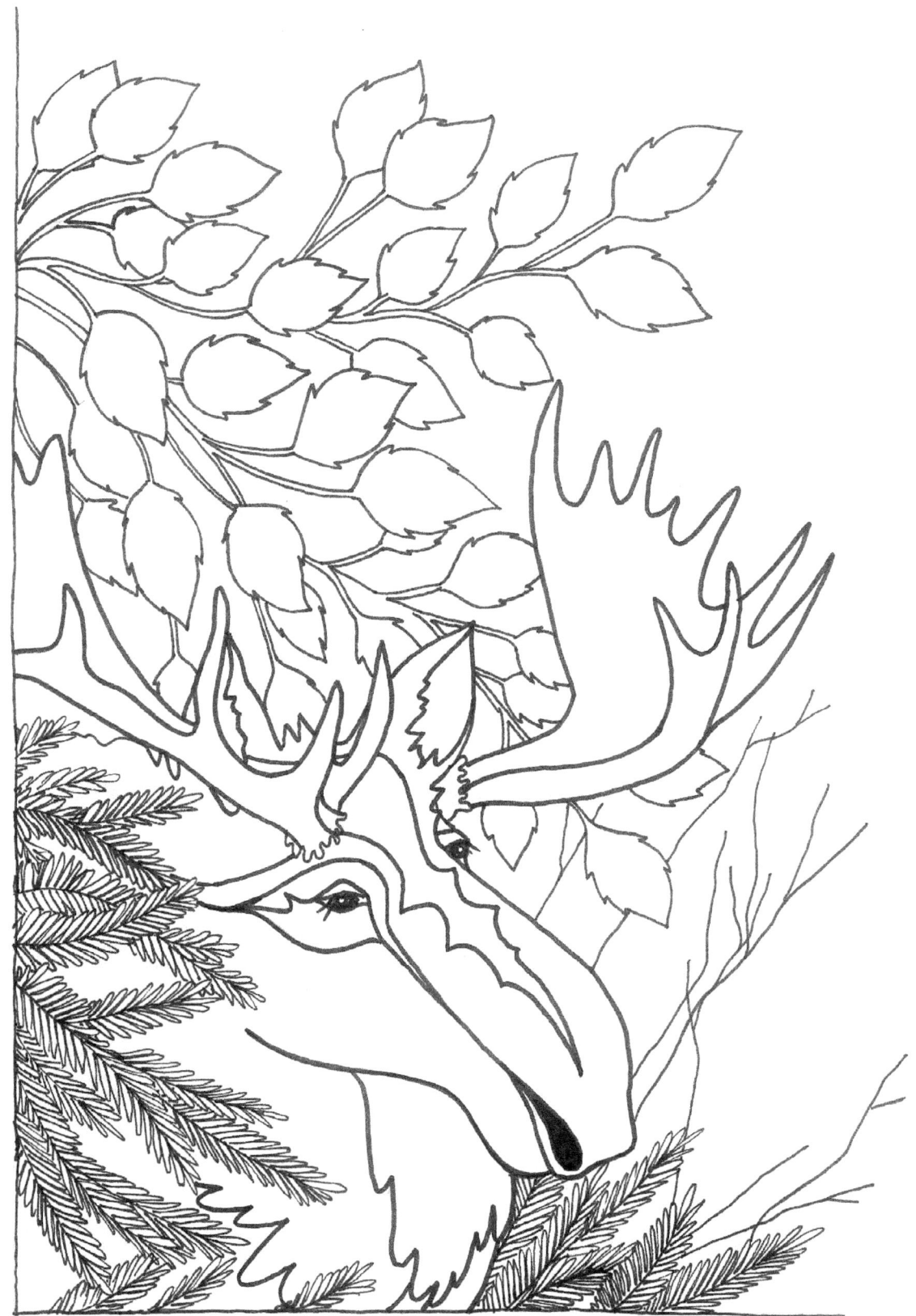

Moose

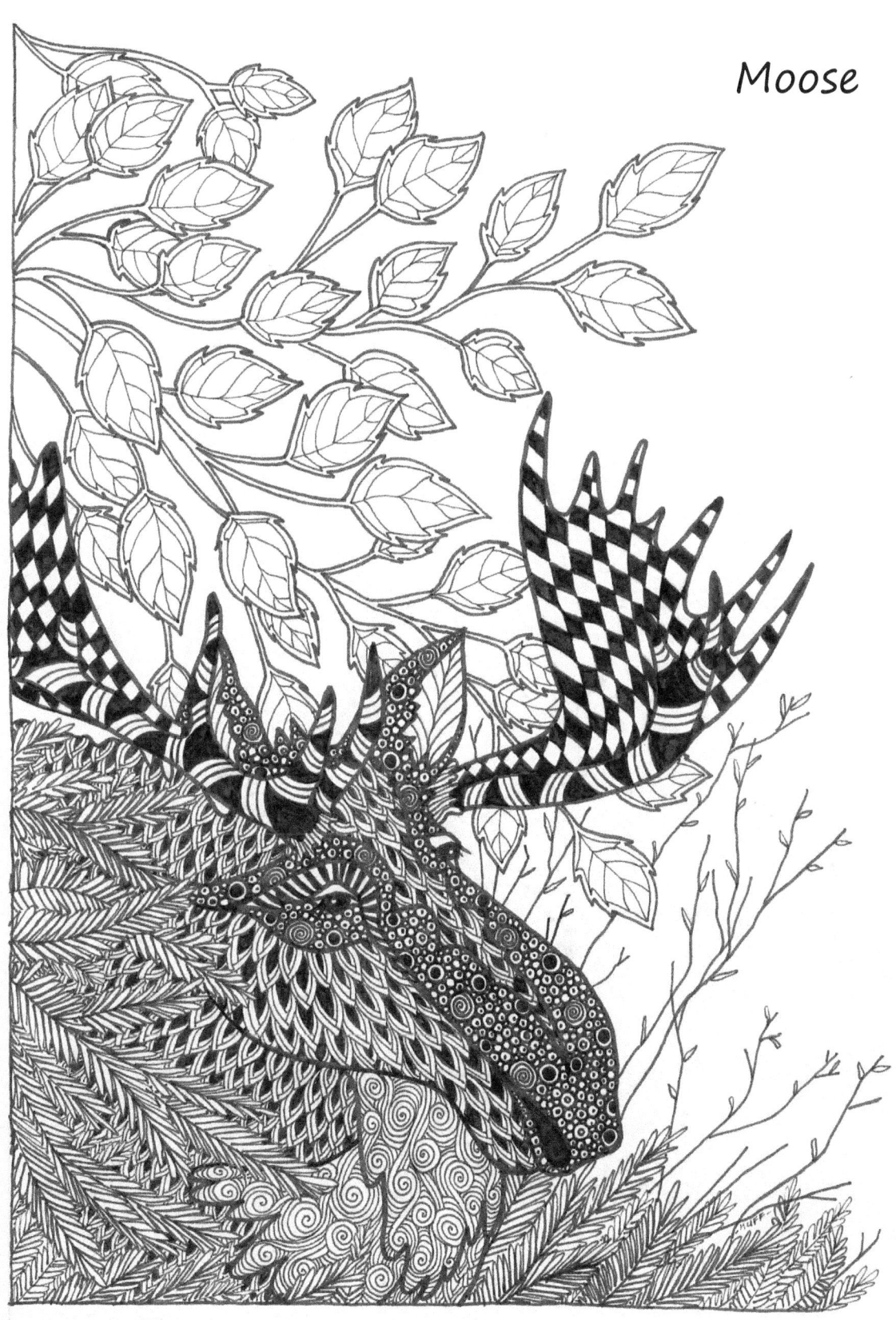

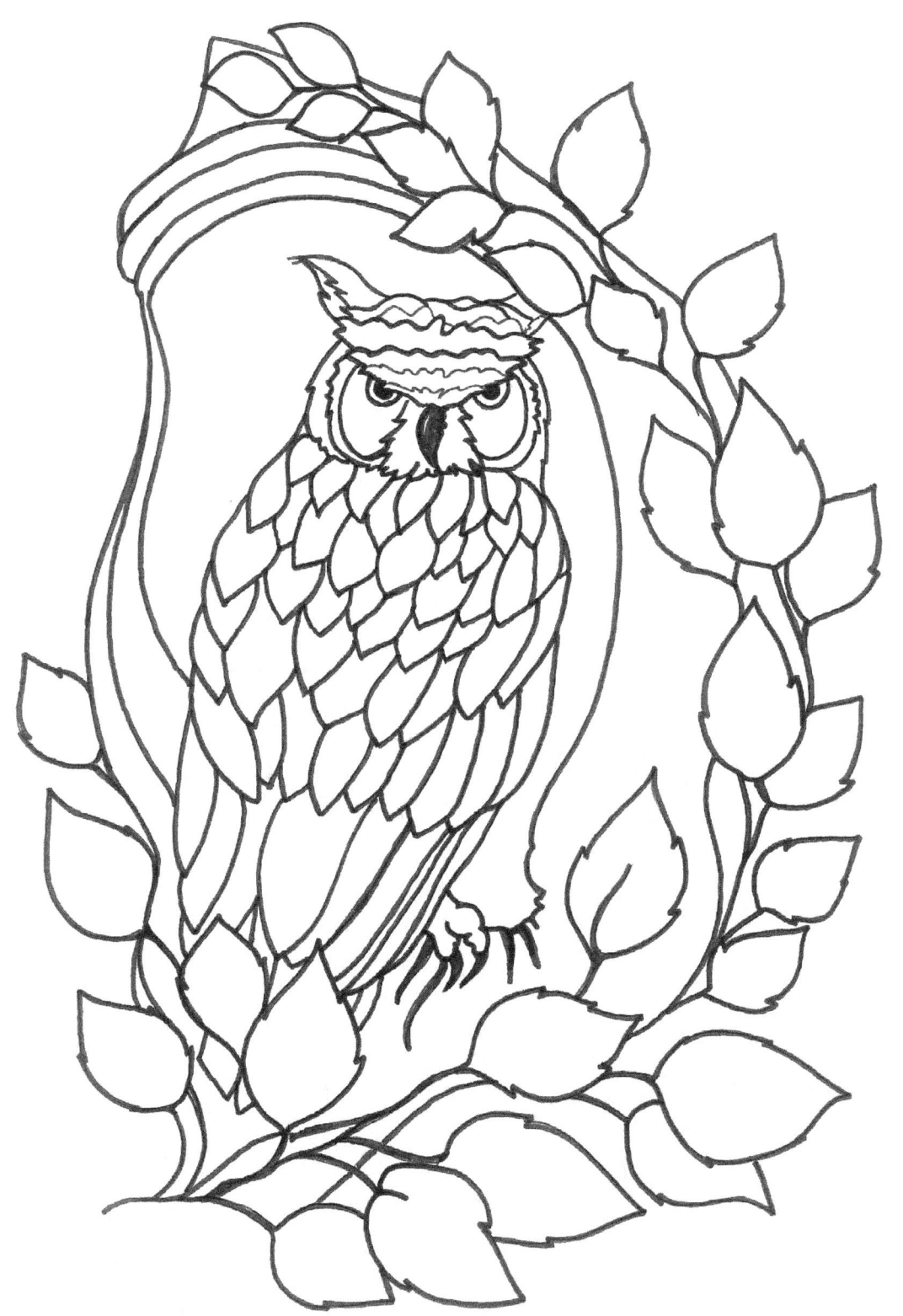

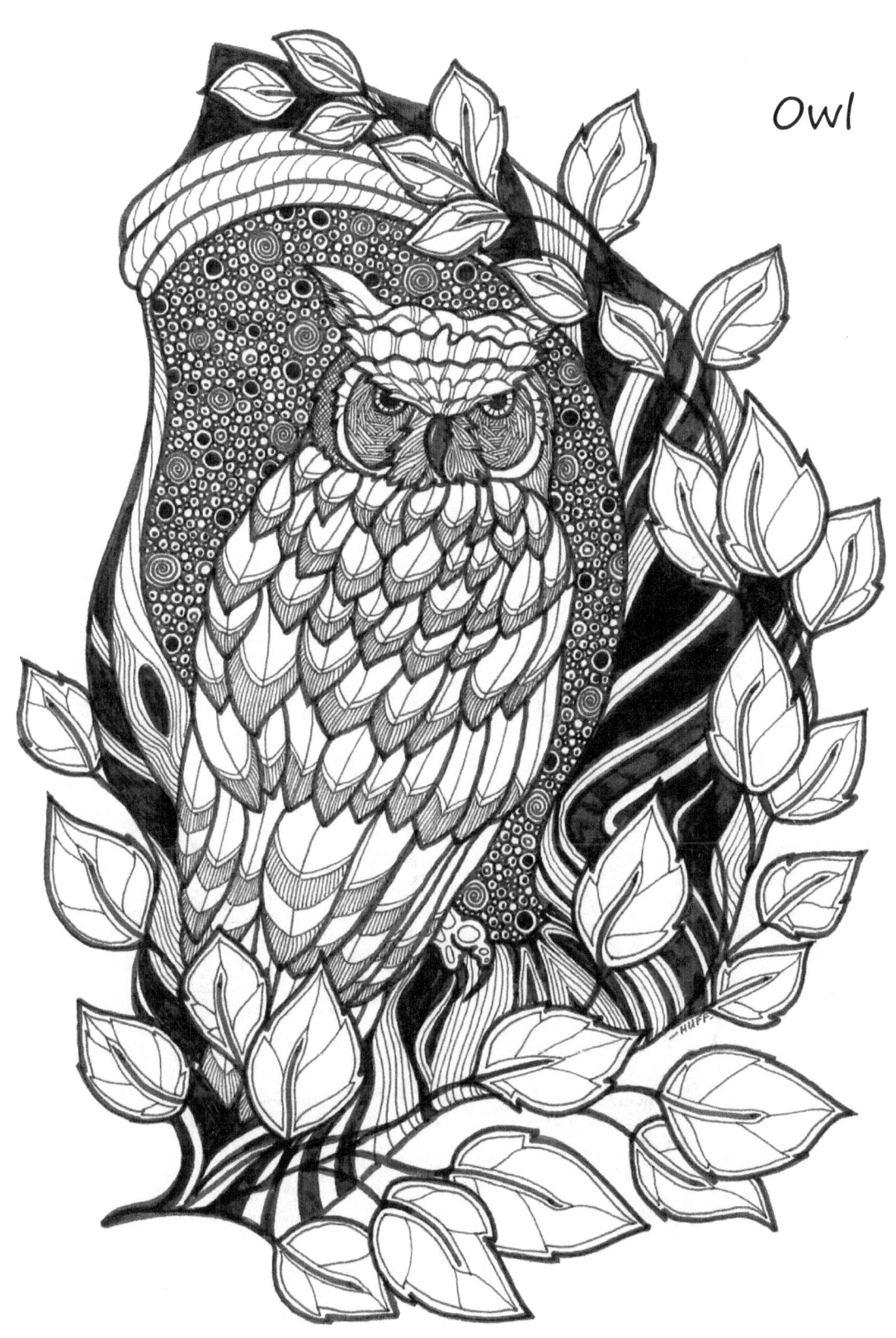

Owl

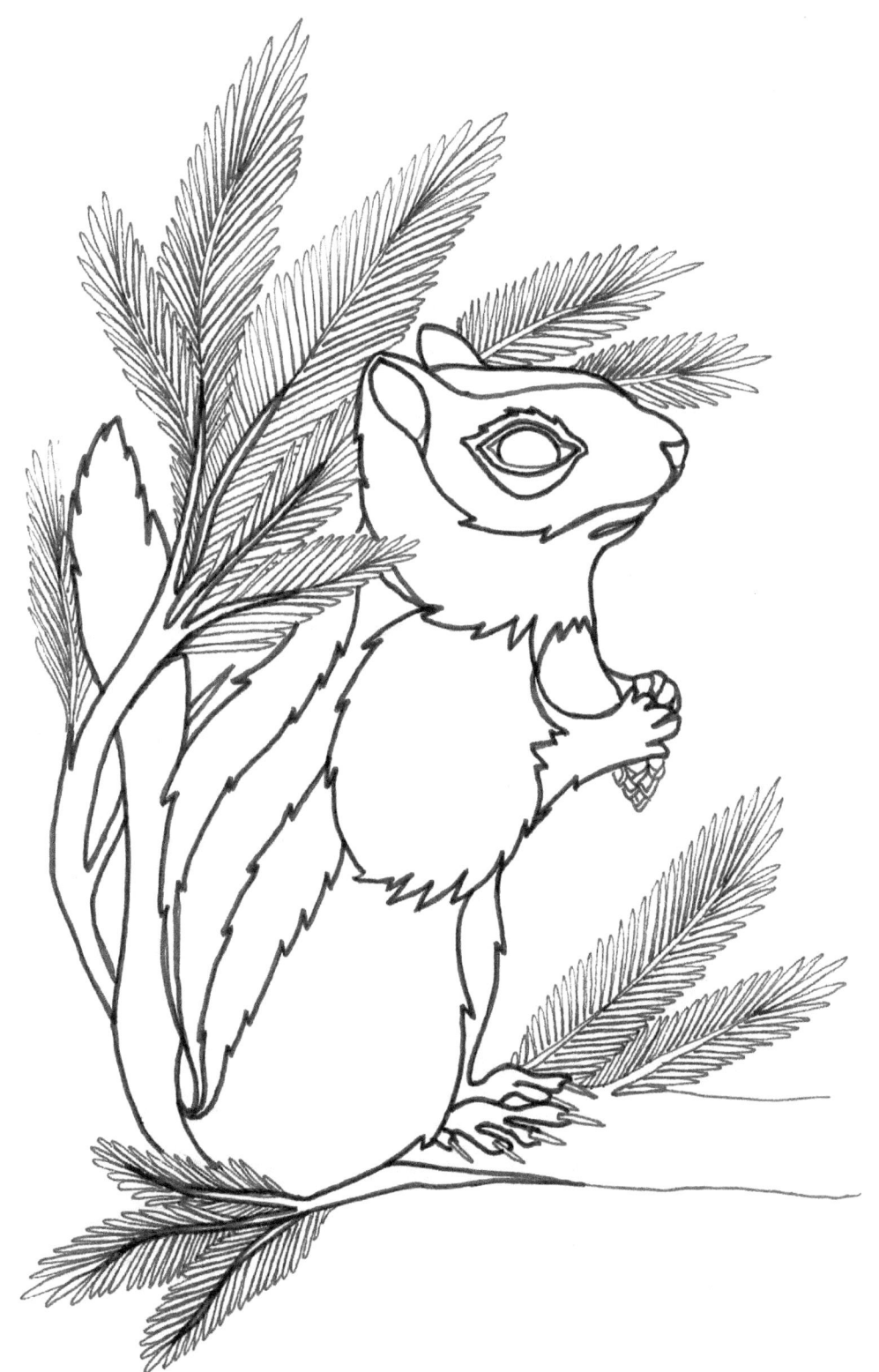

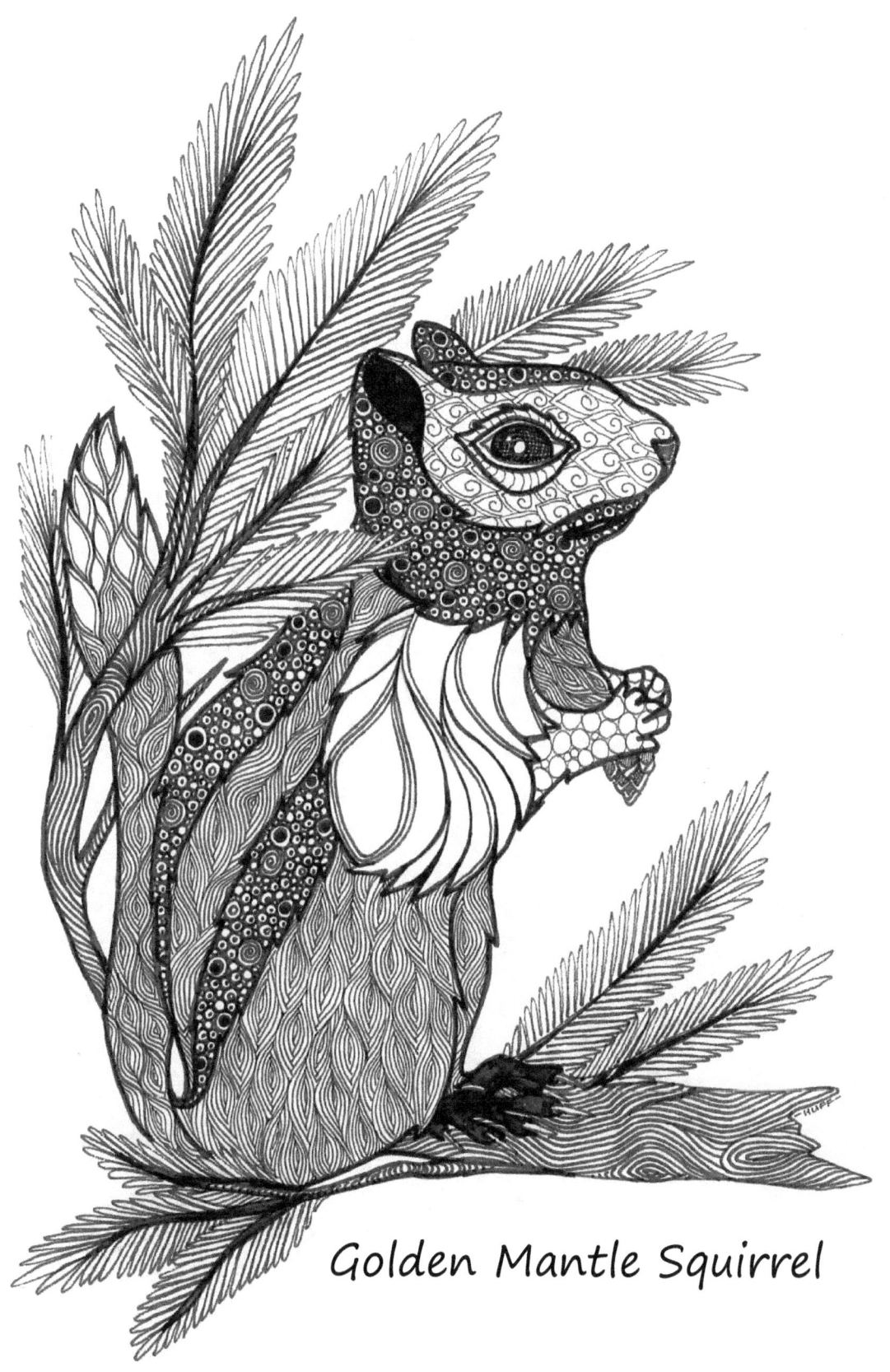

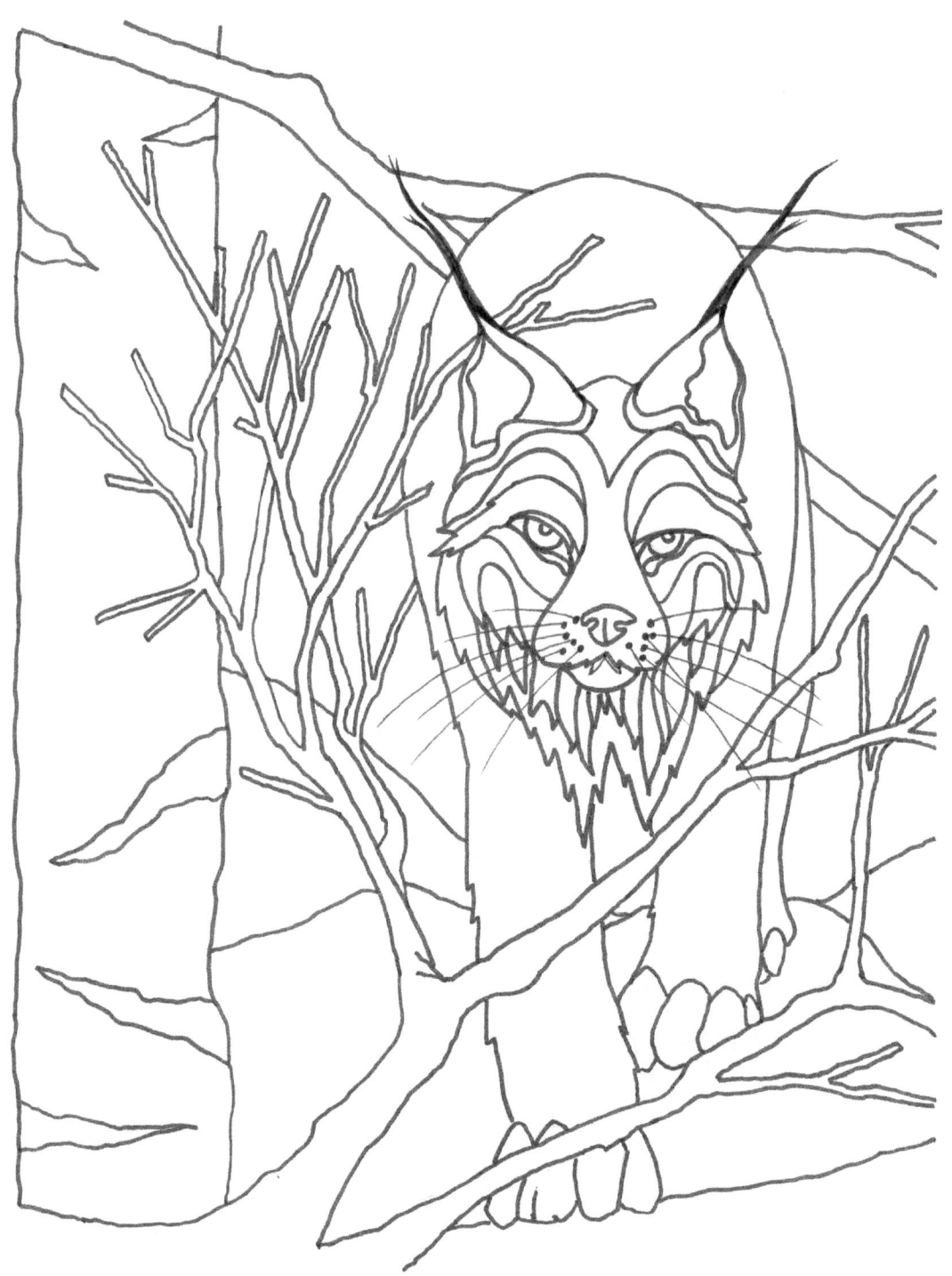

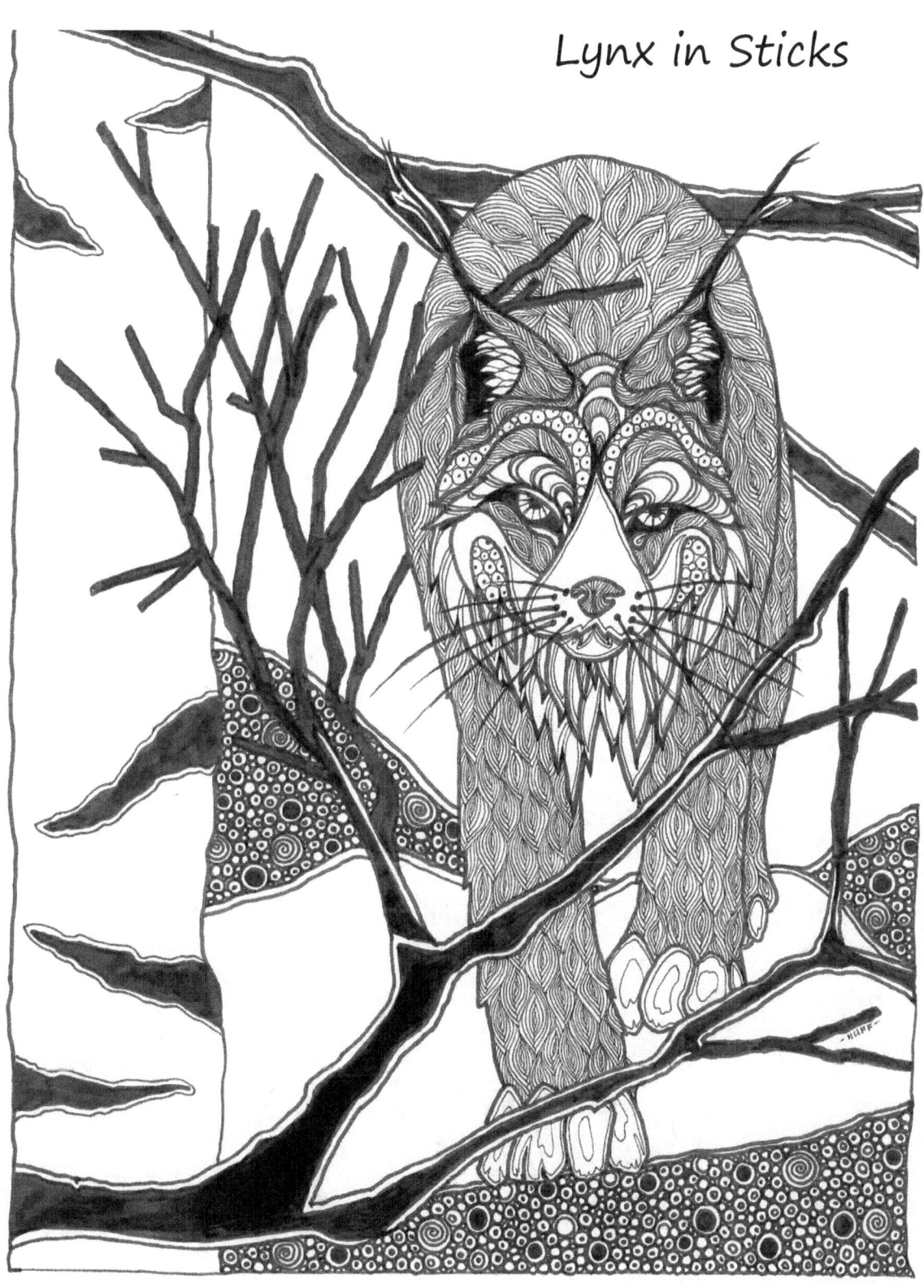
Lynx in Sticks

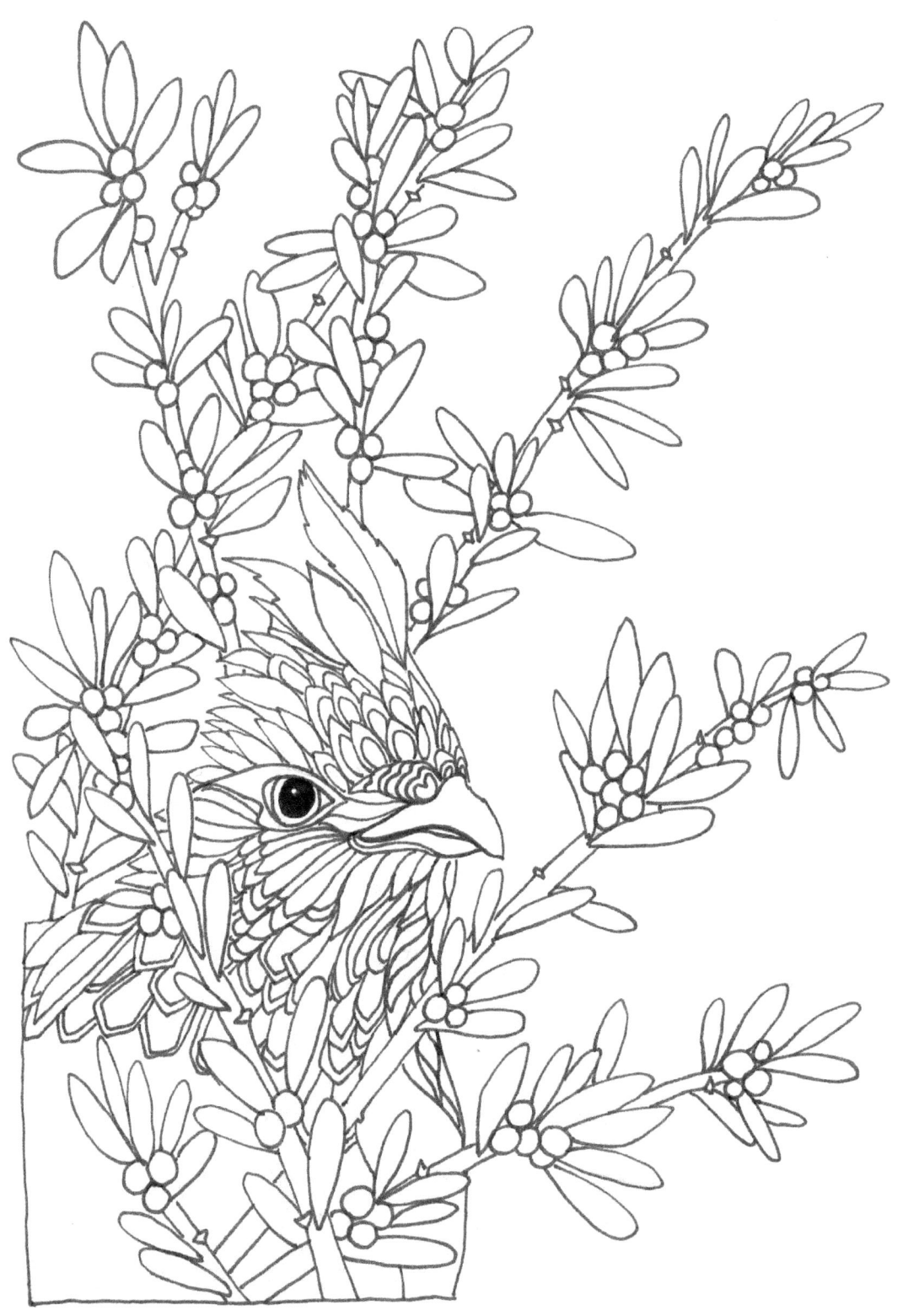

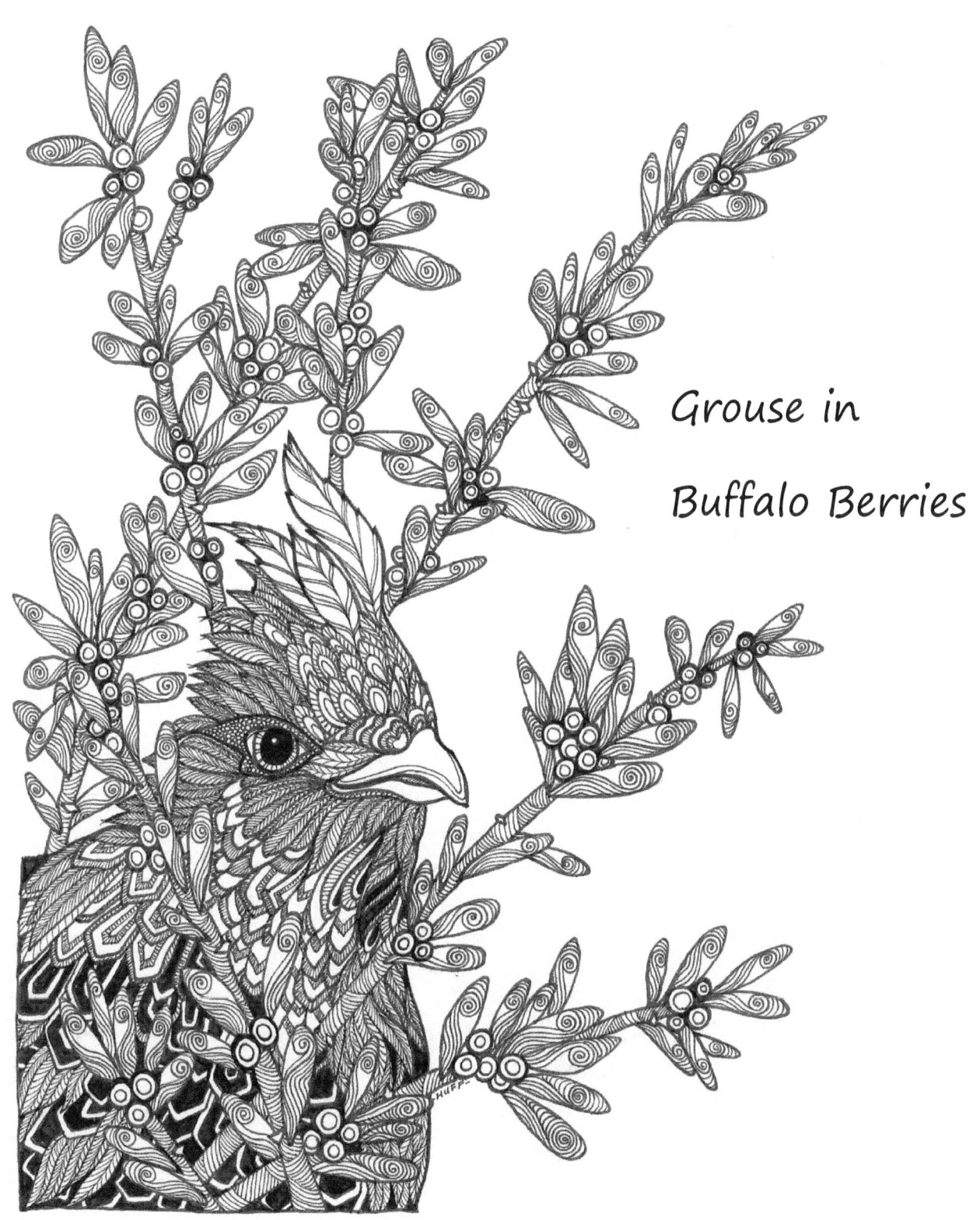

Grouse in Buffalo Berries

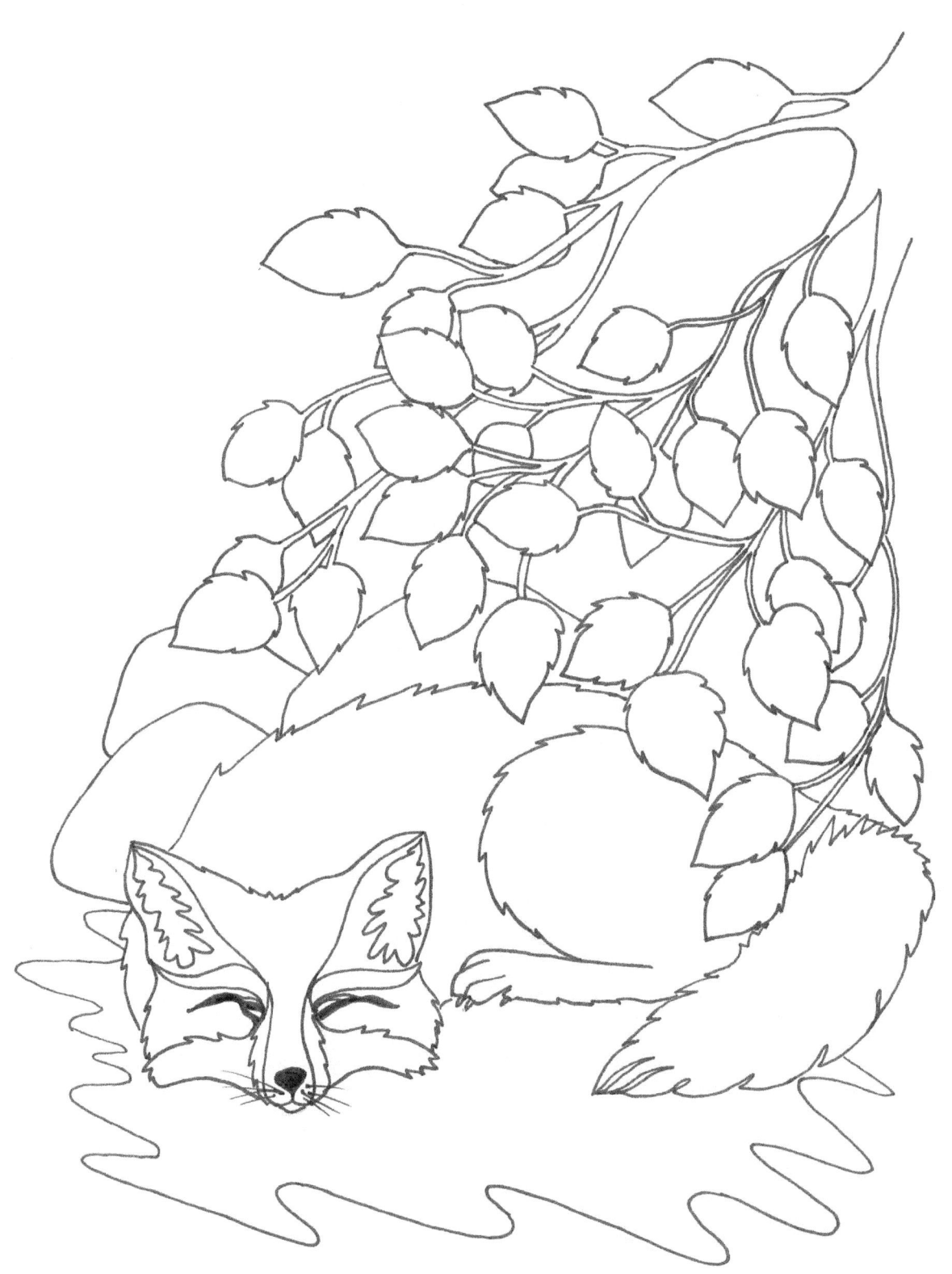

Sleeping Fox

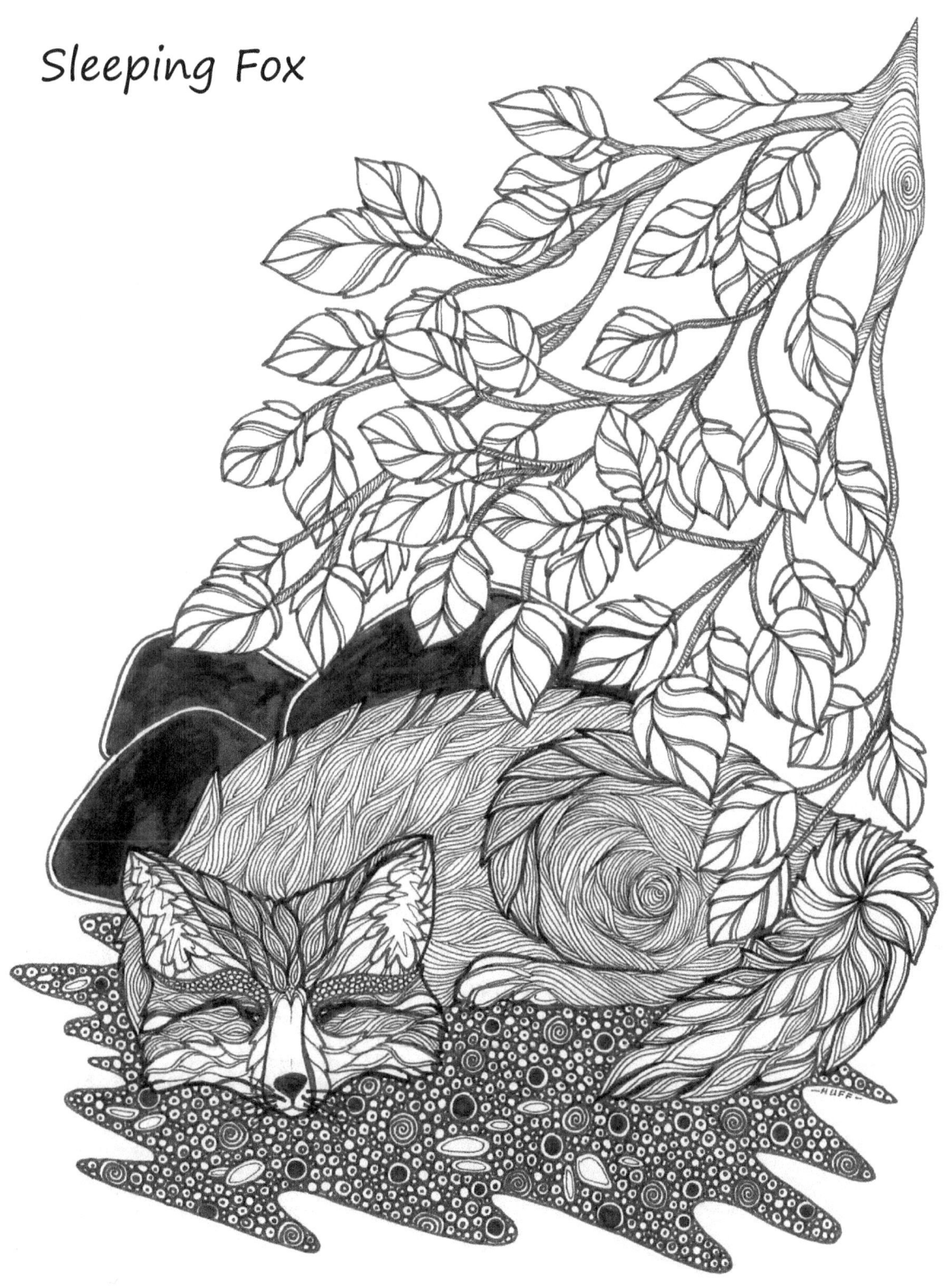

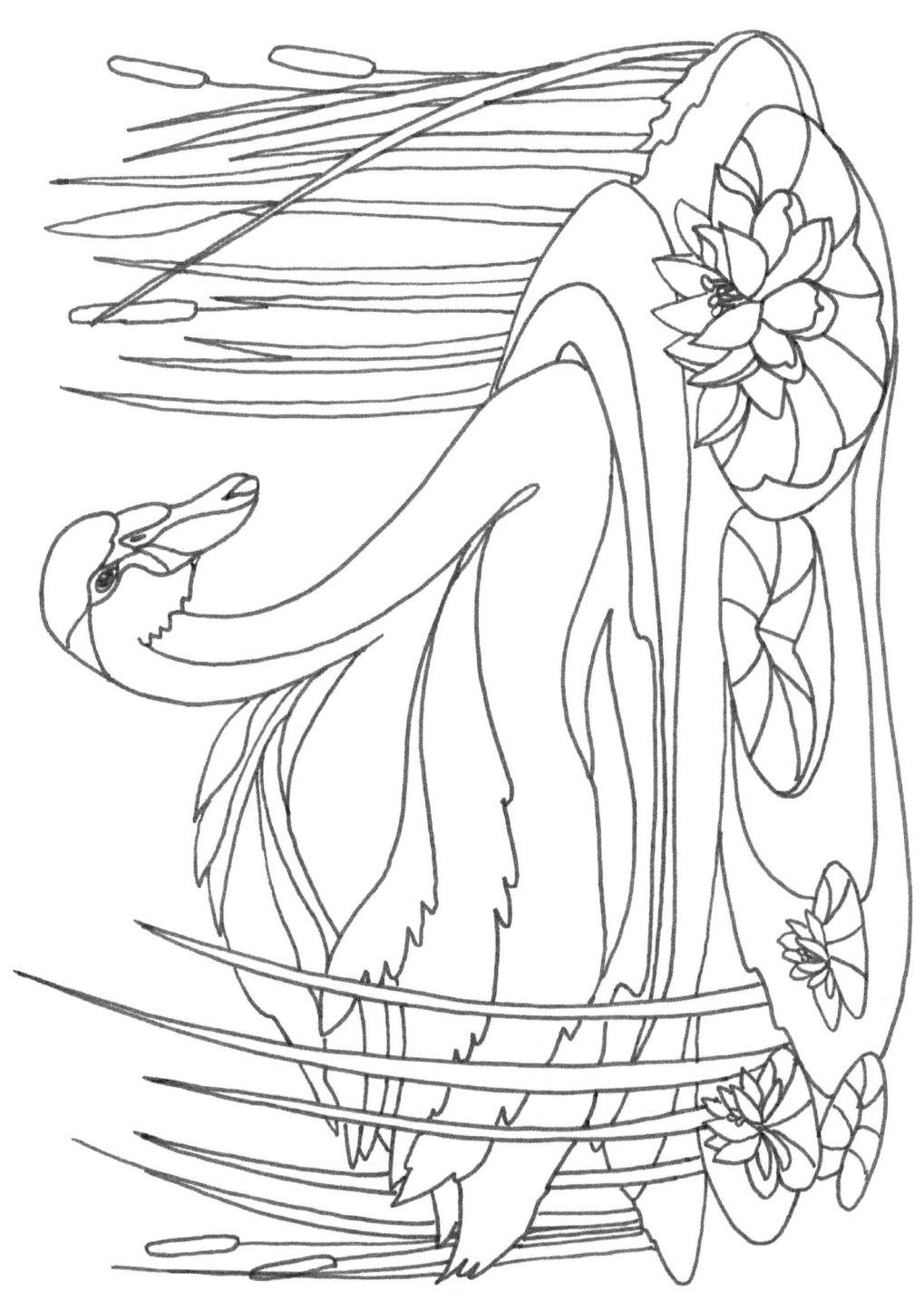

Resting Swan

www.ingramcontent.com/pod-product-compliance
Lightning Source LLC
Chambersburg PA
CBHW062208220526
45470CB00009B/2976